WHAT WOULD HAPPEN IF...

WE HAD TO LIVE ON OTHER PLANETS?

Written by Izzi Howell

Illustrated by Paula Bossio

WORLD BOOK

www.worldbook.com

READING TIPS

This book asks readers to ponder the question *what would happen if we had to live on other planets?* Readers will discover why humans might one day need to move to another planet and the challenges scientists face in finding one that could support life. Use these tips to help readers consider the ripple effects of certain actions and events.

Before Reading

Explain to readers that this book uses cause and effect to help us think about what might happen in the future based on our actions and choices today. It also uses problem and solution to show the challenges we face if we are ever forced to live on other planets. Encourage readers to be on the lookout for examples of cause and effect or problem and solution structures as they explore what would happen if we had to live on other planets.

During Reading

Discuss with readers how some actions and events have multiple causes and others have multiple effects. Likewise, some situations lead to multiple problems and others have multiple solutions. Explain that it can be tricky to keep all of that straight in our minds, so it can be helpful to create a visual guide. Encourage readers to draw and add notes to their own diagrams like those found on pages 31 and 36-37.

After Reading

After finishing the book, discuss with readers how their understandings and opinions about space exploration and taking care of our home planet have changed. Additionally, you can have readers respond to the comprehension questions included on page 46 and can complete the Chain of Events activity on page 47 to further extend the learning.

Visit www.worldbook.com/resources for additional, free educational materials.

There is a glossary of terms on pages 44–45. Terms defined in the glossary are in boldface type that **looks like this** on their first appearance on any spread (two facing pages).

Contents

Home sweet home 4
Earth and space 6
Doomsday dangers 10
Where to go? 16
Blast off! 22
Getting started 26
Next steps 32
Long-term living 36
Conclusion 40
Summary 42
Glossary 44
Review and reflect 46

Home sweet home

Earth is a pretty special planet. Of the 700 quintillion (billion billion) planets believed to exist in the universe, it's the only one with the right conditions for life (as far as we know!).

However, despite Earth's massive value as the only planet that can support life, people haven't been treating it very well. In the past few hundred years, our growing population has been consuming huge amounts of **resources** and producing more pollution and waste than ever before. We may eventually damage our planet so much that we won't be able to live here anymore.

Luckily, we may be able to find a new home among the stars. Scientists believe that it might be possible for humans to survive on another planet or body in our **solar system** or beyond. But where exactly could we live in space—and more importantly, how?!

DID YOU KNOW?

Astronauts, such as Wang Yaping (shown here), are already practicing living in space on **space stations,** such as the Tiangong Space Station.

In 1961, Yuri Gagarin was the first astronaut to travel into outer space.

There has been life on Earth for around 3.7 billion years.

The only other place in space where humans have set foot is the **moon.**

Our solar system is about 5 billion years old.

Many ancient civilizations studied the night sky and made maps of the movements of the stars and planets.

THINK ABOUT IT!

Many people are fascinated by space and our solar system. Why do you think that is?

Earth and space

So, what else is out there in space, besides Earth? Let's start close to home with our **solar system.** Our solar system is made up of eight planets (including Earth) that orbit the sun. It also contains many **moons, dwarf planets, comets,** and **asteroids.**

The four planets closest to the sun are Mercury, Venus, Earth, and Mars. They are small with solid, rocky surfaces.

Farther out, the planets get much bigger! Jupiter and Saturn are known as gas giants because they are mostly made of gas, while Uranus and Neptune are considered to be ice giants.

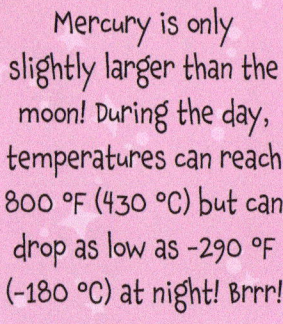

Mercury is only slightly larger than the moon! During the day, temperatures can reach 800 °F (430 °C) but can drop as low as -290 °F (-180 °C) at night! Brrr!

Venus is very similar in size to Earth, but conditions on the planet are very different. It is surrounded by thick clouds of sulfuric acid and has a sweltering average surface temperature of 870 °F (465 °C).

The surface of Mars is dusty, dry, and cold. Scientists have found water on Mars, both frozen as ice and as salty brine on some hillsides.

FUN FACT!

If Earth were as big as a grape, Jupiter would be as big as a basketball!

THINK ABOUT IT!

Other than Earth, which of the planets in our solar system would be the best (or least bad!) place to live? Why?

"What a view!"

Jupiter is more massive than all the other planets in the solar system combined! It doesn't really have a surface ... its stripes and swirly patterns are actually clouds of gas!

Saturn's spectacular rings are made up of fragments of ice and rock. Winds here can reach up to 1,100 miles (1,770 kilometers) per hour.

Uranus is very chilly and windy. Scientists believe that clouds here may smell like rotten eggs! Yuck!

Unsurprisingly, due to its distance from the sun, Neptune is very dark and cold. Sunlight on Earth is about 900 times brighter than sunlight on Neptune.

EARTH AND SPACE

Beyond our **solar system** are countless other planets known as **exoplanets.** So far, we have mostly discovered exoplanets in a small area of the Milky Way, the **galaxy** in which our solar system is located. However, scientists are sure that there are many more exoplanets out there, some of which may be similar to Earth.

Exoplanets are so far away that it's very hard to see them directly. Instead, scientists look for the impact that exoplanets have on the stars around them. The **gravity** of exoplanets can pull on the light from stars and make it wobble. Scientists can also spot dips in the amount of light released by a star, which means that an exoplanet is crossing the star's path!

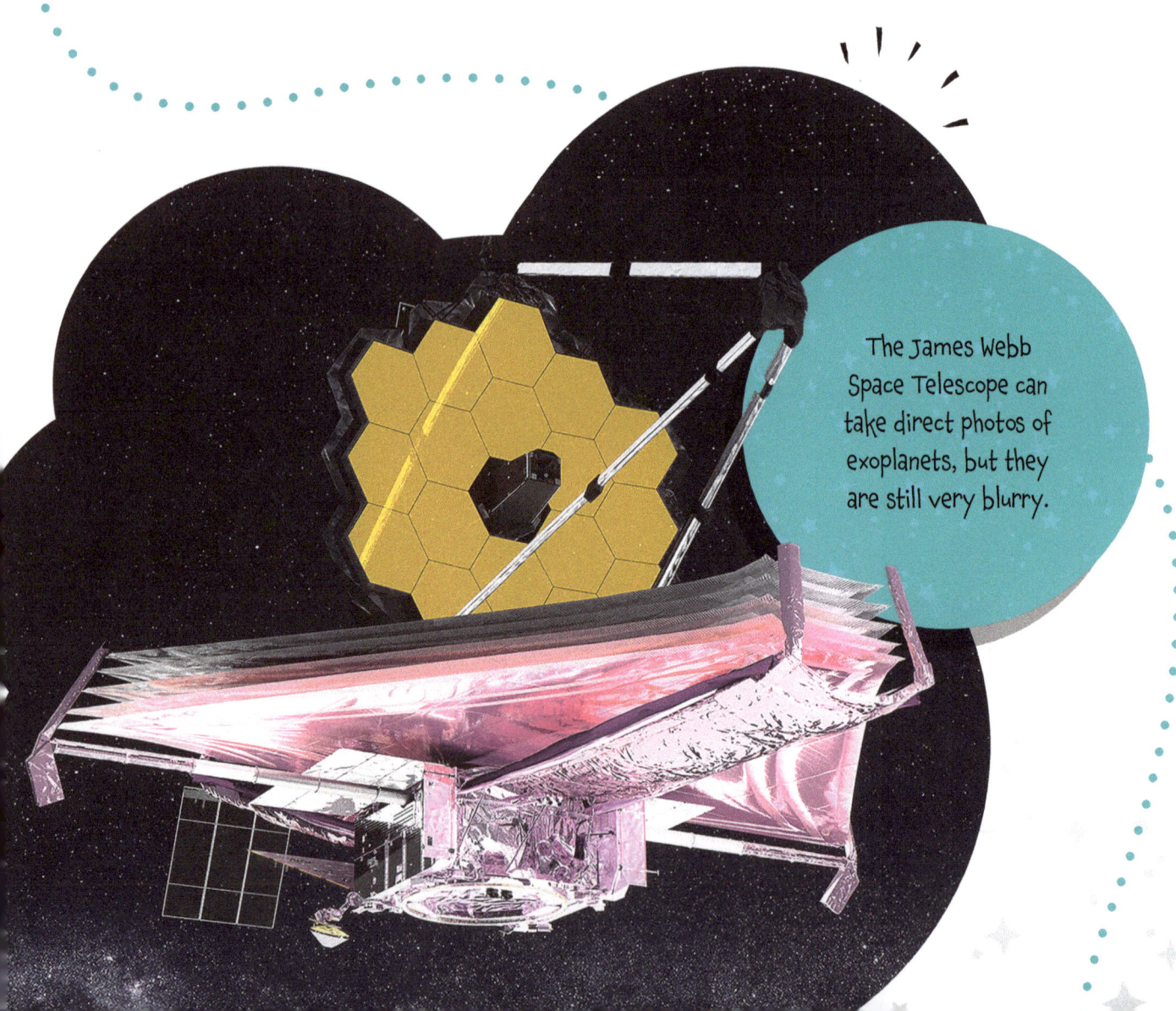

The James Webb Space Telescope can take direct photos of exoplanets, but they are still very blurry.

Once scientists know where an exoplanet is, they can use powerful space telescopes to learn more about it. Recently, space telescopes have been analyzing light from certain exoplanets to discover which **molecules** are present in their **atmospheres**. Scientists can use this information to predict what conditions might be like on the exoplanet.

Too much lava for me!

The surface of the exoplanet 55 Cancri e is totally covered in molten lava. If you were brave enough to go down to its surface, the sky above you would sparkle, thanks to tiny **particles** of silicon in its atmosphere.

Hi! I'm Elisa Quintana. I'm an American astronomer who studies exoplanets and how to find them. During my career, I've helped discover lots of interesting exoplanets. One of the most interesting is Kepler-186f. This exoplanet is about the same size as Earth and about the same distance from the star in its solar system. This means that it might have liquid water on its surface! There are still so many more exoplanets to discover ... Maybe one day soon we'll find one where humans could live!

FUN FACT!

There are actually more planets than stars in the Milky Way!

Doomsday dangers

Earth has been our home for millions of years, through good times and bad. We've managed to survive this far, so it's pretty unlikely that we'd have to look for a new home anytime soon. However, there are some serious threats that might put our planet at risk.

Up until the late 1700's and 1800's, humans didn't have a big impact on our planet. The world population was much smaller. People used far fewer **resources,** because they didn't need such **fossil fuels** as coal, natural gas, or oil to power vehicles or machines, or such materials as metal to make large numbers of goods.

However, during the Industrial Revolution in the late 1700's, many countries around the world started using new machines powered by coal. They built factories where large amounts of items could be made by machines very quickly and easily. We started using more resources than ever before.

Open coal mines like this one destroy huge areas of natural countryside.

DID YOU KNOW?
There's less than 50 years' worth of oil left on Earth if we continue to use it at the same rate.

FUN FACT!

In 1700 (before the Industrial Revolution), about 3 million tons (2.7 million metric tons) of coal were mined in Britain each year. By 1830 (during the Industrial Revolution), that amount had jumped to 30 million tons (27.2 million metric tons)!

Pumps like this are used to extract oil from deep underground.

Since then, our use of natural resources has rocketed out of control. We extract so many resources from our planet that we may soon run out. If we used up all Earth's resources, we would find it hard to make, build, or power anything.

THINK ABOUT IT!

Do you think every country around the world uses the same quantity of resources? Why do you think this is? Do you think this is fair?

DOOMSDAY DANGERS

Using so many **fossil fuels** has created another threat to our planet. When fossil fuels are burned, they release greenhouse gases. These gases gather in Earth's **atmosphere** and trap heat from the sun, which makes the surface of our planet much hotter. This is known as **global warming.**

But wait, that's not all! Our climate isn't just getting hotter ... it's also changing. Global warming affects normal weather patterns on Earth, such as rainfall, and increases the chances of extreme weather, such as **drought,** storms, and heat waves.

DID YOU KNOW?

The eight warmest years on record have all taken place since 2014.

Many animals struggle to find enough food or water to survive during periods of drought.

Many people around the world are already suffering the effects of global warming and **climate change**. **Crops** can't grow because of drought, which leads to food shortages. Many coastlines are being flooded because of changing rainfall patterns. Wildfires are destroying natural ecosystems *and* towns and cities. If we don't get global warming and climate change under control, our planet's weather could become so extreme and dangerous that it would be very hard to continue living here.

This village in the Philippines has been flooded by unusually heavy monsoon rains.

DID YOU KNOW?
Scientists believe that by 2050, plastic will outweigh all of the fish in the oceans.

Humans are also damaging our planet with pollution. In many places, garbage and waste are poisoning the soil, water, and air. This pollution kills many plants and animals and can lead to serious health problems, and even death, for humans. If we continue to poison Earth by using it as a trash can, it may become too toxic for us to live here.

DOOMSDAY DANGERS

Humans are responsible for many of the potential threats to our planet, but there are also some dangers that are totally out of our control!

Every year, many tiny meteorites fall to Earth from space and are barely noticed by anyone. However, very rarely, much larger **asteroids** hit our planet with devastating consequences. For example, scientists believe that the collision of a massive asteroid led to the extinction of the dinosaurs 66 million years ago. The crash created a huge amount of dust, which blocked sunlight from reaching Earth. Our climate changed so much that most animals, including the dinosaurs, couldn't survive. In the very unlikely event that an asteroid of a similar size hit Earth again, our planet might become uninhabitable.

DID YOU KNOW?

The asteroid that led to the extinction of the dinosaurs was about 50 miles (81 km) wide. That's about nine times the height of Mount Everest!

Watch out! I can't stop!

Another improbable but catastrophic event would be a supervolcanic eruption. These supersized eruptions are far more powerful than the normal eruptions that take place on Earth every day. They have the potential to cover entire continents in ash and make Earth's climate much colder for years and years.

Unexpected changes to the sun could also have a huge impact on our planet. Much less or much more solar energy could freeze our planet or leave us scorched. However, scientists don't believe that this is likely to happen.

THINK ABOUT IT!

What do you think is a greater risk to our planet—humans or a natural disaster? Why?

Sorry!

Where to go?

As far as we know, Earth is unique in the universe in having just the right conditions for life. But what exactly are these conditions?

I'm special!

Distance

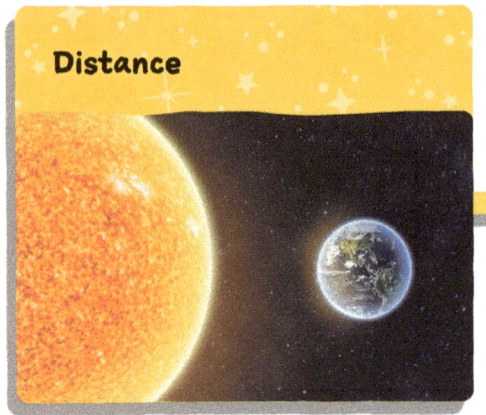

A planet or another body in space needs to be the right distance from a star for living things to survive. Too close, and they'd get too hot … too far away, and they'd freeze! This distance is known as the "habitable zone" of a star.

Water

Living things need access to liquid water. The water needs to be liquid, since most plants and animals can't melt frozen water before they drink it. Being in the habitable zone makes it much more likely for a planet or other body to have liquid water on its surface.

Atmosphere

Without Earth's **atmosphere**, we'd be lost! Our atmosphere protects us from dangerous **radiation** from space, keeps us warm, and traps oxygen-rich air for us to breathe.

Energy

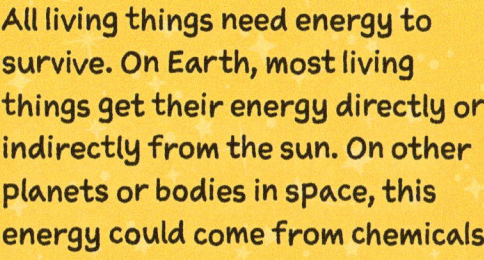

All living things need energy to survive. On Earth, most living things get their energy directly or indirectly from the sun. On other planets or bodies in space, this energy could come from chemicals.

Elements

All living things on Earth are made of certain building block **elements**, including carbon and nitrogen. These elements are common across space, but Earth is the only spot where they've come together to create life!

THINK ABOUT IT!

Time and luck were also important factors in the development of life on Earth. Why do you think that is?

Hurry up, life, I've been waiting for AGES!

It's incredible luck that Earth meets all these requirements. Some planets in our **solar system** and beyond have one or two of these conditions, but they have other issues that make them unsuitable as a potential home for humans.

Mercury—I receive too much **radiation** from the sun, and temperatures on my surface are too extreme.

Venus—I'm too hot, and the **pressure** on my surface is much too high. I also don't contain any water in any form.

Jupiter and Saturn—We don't have solid surfaces, so there'd be nowhere for you to live! Sorry!

Uranus and Neptune—We're much too far from the sun. Brrr!!!

WHERE TO GO?

However, there is one potential candidate in our solar system—Mars. Mars is similar to Earth in many ways. It has a solid, rocky surface that looks a lot like Earth (but without any plants!). Very small amounts of liquid water sometimes form on its surface, and ice caps are found at its poles.

Ice inside a crater on Mars.

Despite its similarities, humans wouldn't be able to live on Mars without a lot of assistance. It's much colder than Earth and has less of an **atmosphere**. This means that we wouldn't be able to breathe without assistance. If you want a sneak peek, skip ahead to pages 26–31 to see how humans might be able to live on Mars!

FUN FACT!

Like Earth, Mars also has seasons, weather, and volcanoes!

DID YOU KNOW?

Scientists believe that Mars used to be a much warmer, wetter planet, so life may have existed there long ago!

Mars isn't our only option! Scientists are considering other planets and bodies as potential sites for human colonization, including Saturn's **moon** Titan and the TRAPPIST-1 system of **exoplanets**.

Humans have managed to "visit" Titan, in a manner of speaking! The Huygens **probe** landed on its surface in 2005 and sent back important data about its structure, winds, and atmosphere.

Titan holds the special title of being the only moon in our **solar system** with a thick **atmosphere**. This means that we'd be able to walk around easily on its surface (if we were wearing an oxygen mask and a suit to keep warm!).

Liquid methane forms a type of "water cycle" on Titan, flowing in rivers and seas across its surface, evaporating up into clouds in the atmosphere, and then falling back to the ground as rain. This could be a useful fuel for human settlers. And last, but certainly not least, Titan has a massive ocean hidden underneath its surface, believed to be mostly liquid water! Hooray!

Home sweet home?

FUN FACT!

The Huygens probe even took a photo of the surface of Titan!

WHERE TO GO?

Scientists are also investigating farther afield. One site of interest is TRAPPIST-1—a small, distant star orbited by seven exoplanets. Four of TRAPPIST-1's planets are in its habitable zone, which means that liquid water could be found on their surfaces. We still have much more to learn about the TRAPPIST-1 system but may make a breakthrough at any time thanks to data gathered by the James Webb Space Telescope.

An artist's impression of TRAPPIST-1e. This exoplanet is believed to have a solid, rocky surface.

THINK ABOUT IT!
Which of these worlds would you most like to visit or live on? Why?

Next stop... Mars!

Blast off!

Now that we've got some possible destinations, let's look at how we'd actually make a home in space. First things first—how would we get there?

Wherever we go, we'd need to use rocket-powered spacecraft to transport people and supplies. We'd probably need a whole fleet of spacecraft to fit in everything we'd need! In the case of a relatively close destination like Mars, the journey would only take about seven months. A trip to Titan would take longer—roughly seven years.

However, once we moved outside of our **solar system**, travel would become much trickier. The TRAPPIST-1 system is 39 **light-years** from our solar system, or 229 trillion miles (369 trillion kilometers). Even the fastest modern spacecraft would take more than 800,000 years to get there. And many other potentially habitable **exoplanets** are even farther away!

Are we almost there yet?

Obviously, we're going to need faster spacecraft! At the moment, spacecraft are powered by fuel or sometimes electric energy. However, scientists believe that other types of technology could be used to make spacecraft travel even faster. One day, we might be able to power a ship using nuclear energy, solar power, or even lasers!

This is an artist's impression of a laser-powered spacecraft.

THINK ABOUT IT!

Get creative and design a new type of superspeed rocket. It doesn't matter if your idea is silly. Some of the biggest ideas in science today were once thought to be ridiculous!

DID YOU KNOW?

Even if we could travel at the speed of light, getting to the TRAPPIST-1 system would take 39 years! Unfortunately, scientists don't believe that humans could survive traveling at the speed of light, even if spacecraft were able to.

BLAST OFF!

The human life span is also an important consideration when it comes to longer trips. We wouldn't want to send off young astronauts and then have them arrive as elderly people unable to do tough physical work! Some trips may even take significantly longer than most humans live.

Scientists have come up with some potential solutions to this problem (although none of them have been tested yet!). One idea is to put settlers into some type of **hibernation** that would put them into suspended animation during the trip. They'd then be woken up once they got to their destination. As well as solving the life span issue, this would also hugely reduce the amount of supplies needed onboard, since no one would be eating or drinking!

Good night! See you in 100 years!

Can you imagine traveling to a new planet "asleep" in one of these pods?

FUN FACT!

One astronaut consumes about 66 pounds (30 kg) of food and water every week!

Another option is a "generation ship," in which many generations of people would be born and die on the ship. Eventually, after many years, the descendants of the original crew would reach their new destination. It sounds simple, but there would be practical issues to overcome, like how to stock the ship with enough supplies for multiple generations, and ethical issues to address, like what it would be like to be born and die in space without ever having a real home planet.

Experiments on **space stations** such as the ISS (International Space Station) are helping us learn more about how the human body is affected by long periods in space. This information could help us plan for such projects as a generation ship.

THINK ABOUT IT!

What do you think it would be like to be born on a generation ship?

Getting started

Once we finally reached our new home in space, how would we survive there? So far, we haven't found any world in space with exactly the same conditions as Earth. Luckily, there are plenty of scientific and technological solutions that could protect us and provide what we need.

Good protective space suits would be must-haves for any **space colonists.** These suits would need to be worn outside, since most worlds in space don't have breathable air, an **atmosphere** thick enough to block **radiation,** the right air **pressure,** or the correct temperature for humans.

Because of this, space colonists would probably spend most of their time inside "habitats"—safe structures that would be pumped full of breathable air at the correct pressure and temperature, and that would protect them from harmful radiation. Colonists would live, sleep, work, and most importantly, take off their heavy space suits inside!

This is an artist's drawing of what a habitat on Mars might look like. Settlers would also bring **rovers** to explore the surface of the planet.

These habitats would be brought over in pieces from Earth and assembled on site by space colonists. It's likely that the different parts of the habitat would be connected by tubes, so that people wouldn't have to suit up to walk to the bathroom! The electricity needed to run the habitats would probably come from solar panels, nuclear power, or even batteries brought from Earth.

THINK ABOUT IT!

Would you rather spend time outside in a space suit exploring a new planet or stay inside a habitat? Why?

FUN FACT!

Scientists have been investigating whether it would be possible to beam power over to a planet from a solar power satellite!

GETTING STARTED

Wait, what about food? **Space colonists** would have to bring large amounts of food with them for the journey and the first weeks and months of settlement. However, in the long run, they'd have to be able to grow and produce their own food in the new world, since it wouldn't be possible to survive forever on food imported from Earth.

Scientists have suggested that silkworms could be a good source of protein for long space journeys. Silkworms would be easy to rear in space, meaning that astronauts wouldn't have to bring as much food from home.

FUN FACT!

Sunflowers, tulips, peas, cucumbers, and bok choy have all been grown in space!

Since there is no life on other planets, space colonists would bring plants, and possibly animals, to raise for food. Their habitats would have indoor farms where they could safely grow all the food they'd ever need! At the moment, scientists are studying how plants grow in space. Their research will show us how best to produce food on other worlds.

"Who's hungry?"

Hi! I'm Liu Hanlong. I'm a Chinese scientist who recently led a project to grow the first plants on the **moon!** We sent different types of seeds to the surface on a lunar lander. The seeds can't grow directly on the moon's surface, since it's too cold and there's too much solar **radiation.** However, inside the safety of a closed chamber, the seeds sprouted and grew, just like on Earth!

THINK ABOUT IT!

Space colonists might not be able to grow and make every food from Earth on another planet. Which food would you miss the most if you couldn't bring it with you?

Astronaut Serena Auñón-Chancellor harvests kale and lettuce grown on the ISS. Some of these leaves are used for research, while others are eaten by crew members as a snack!

GETTING STARTED

Scientists will only consider building settlements in locations with water on their surface, so any new world would have available water. However, this water might need to be processed or treated before colonists could use it. It's likely that **space colonists** won't have access to large amounts of safe water, so they'll need to make sure they use it efficiently (and not leave the faucet running while they are brushing their teeth!). Habitats will be designed with water recycling systems so that colonists can make the most of every last drop!

THINK ABOUT IT!

What do you do to save water at home and school? Would any of these ideas help save water on another planet?

What would space colonists need to get started in space?

- Safe air to breathe
- Protection from extreme temperatures
- The correct air **pressure**
- Protection from solar **radiation**

→ While exploring the planet's surface, colonists would wear protective space suits.

→ Eventually, colonists would assemble protective habitats with controlled pressure, temperature, and air inside, where they could hang out without wearing their space suits.

- Food

→ To begin with, colonists would eat food brought from Earth.

→ Later, they'd set up farms inside the habitats where they could grow and raise plants and animals for food.

- Water

→ Water would be gathered from the planet. It would possibly need to be processed before use.

Next steps

Okay, so we've got food, water, and shelter. Now it's time to make the most of our new home in space and the **resources** it has to offer!

While it's possible that some spacecraft may be able to return to Earth for more supplies, this would depend on the distance from our new home and the state we left Earth in! Let's imagine that other than the supplies the **space colonists** brought with them, everything else will have to come from their new planet.

Luckily, many planets and bodies in space are rich in useful resources. For example, Titan (see page 20) is covered in rivers and lakes of natural gas, which could easily be collected to use as fuel. Scientists also expect to find many types of metal **ores,** including iron, which can be used for construction and rare earth **elements,** which are used for electronics.

DID YOU KNOW?
Titan has hundreds of times more liquid fuel on its surface than all of the oil and natural gas on Earth.

This proposed lunar base is built of a tube transported from Earth, covered with an inflatable dome and layers of lunar soil.

Even less "valuable" resources can be extremely useful. Water can be broken down into hydrogen and oxygen, which are used to make rocket fuel. Soil from the planet's surface could be used as a building material!

Hi! I'm Ding Lieyun. I'm a Chinese scientist who is working on a project to build a base on the **moon!** Instead of carrying heavy materials from Earth, we'll be using local materials to build our base. Our 3D printers will print blocks using moon soil. They'll slot together a bit like LEGO bricks! To make things even easier, we'll use a robot to build structures from the bricks. I can't wait to see it in place!

NEXT STEPS

One of the big pluses of having a home somewhere else in space would be creating a base for space exploration. We'd be much closer to areas that we haven't yet had the chance to explore in person, due to their distance from Earth. Rockets and spacecraft would also be able to set off with full fuel tanks, allowing them to get much deeper into space.

So far, we've only been able to observe most of the planets, **moons,** and other bodies in our **solar system** with **probes.** If we had a base on another planet or moon, **space colonists** could easily take trips to more distant parts of the solar system and take a look for themselves!

The JUICE probe is set to explore Jupiter's icy moons—Ganymede, Europa, and Callisto. Scientists believe that these moons may have seas of liquid water beneath their icy crust. Maybe one day, we'll be able to return in person and take a swim!

If we set up a colony on Mars, one of the top candidates for further exploration would be the **asteroid** belt between Mars and Jupiter. This area is home to most of the asteroids in our solar system. Many people would like to be able to visit the asteroid belt because asteroids are extremely rich in **resources.** Some contain huge amounts of metal, precious stones, and water that can be converted to fuel (see previous page).

FUN FACT!

The asteroid 16 Psyche, which is found between Mars and Jupiter, has a massive core of iron, nickel, and gold worth an unbelievable $10 quadrillion! That's enough to make everyone on Earth a billionaire!

THINK ABOUT IT!

Which area of our solar system or beyond would you most want to explore and why?

Long-term living

In the short term, living on another planet would involve finding solutions to keep us safe and alive, such as building structures and finding useful **resources**. However, we'd have to think about our long-term plans as well, including making the planet easier to live on and ensuring our way of life is sustainable.

Scientists have discussed the possibility of **terraforming** planets and other bodies in space. This means changing and modifying them to make them more like Earth. This process might make it possible for us to explore the surface without space suits and grow plants outside habitats!

Problem

Mars doesn't have a protective **magnetic field**, which means that **particles** from the sun are able to blast away its **atmosphere**.

Solution

Place a giant magnetic shield between Mars and the sun.

Consequence

Mars's atmosphere would build up again. A thicker atmosphere would increase surface temperature and **pressure**, making it more suitable for humans. Some of its ice caps would melt, releasing more liquid water for us to use.

Problem

Mars doesn't have enough breathable oxygen in its atmosphere.

Solution

Introduce microorganisms that carry out photosynthesis.

Consequence

The microorganisms would convert carbon dioxide from Mars's atmosphere into oxygen as part of their **photosynthesis**. The oxygen would be released into the atmosphere.

Problem

Mars has a very thin atmosphere due to its lack of magnetic field (as we've already seen).

Solution

Introduce greenhouse gases from different sources to create a greenhouse effect on the planet. Water vapor could come from melting Mars's ice caps, or carbon dioxide could be extracted from carbon-rich minerals on its surface.

Consequence

The greenhouse effect makes Mars's atmosphere thicker and traps heat from the sun. The surface of the planet becomes warmer.

LONG-TERM LIVING

So far, scientists have only come up with theories about **terraforming.** They'd need to do lots more experiments and research to check that it would work. It's also unlikely that we'd be able to carry out any of these complex projects with current technology. For now, it's an interesting idea—but maybe one day in the future, it just might be possible!

Considering that human activity is currently putting Earth in danger, we'd also need to consider how our arrival would affect our new home in space. We'd need to think about how to use **resources** sustainably and how to prevent waste and pollution.

This is what Mars might look like after terraforming.

Now

After terraforming

There's already a lot of garbage from broken satellites and spacecraft in orbit around Earth.

DID YOU KNOW?

There are more than 27,000 large pieces of space debris in orbit around Earth and many more smaller ones.

There's also a lot that we don't know about how the human body would cope with being in space. Being in places with less **gravity** can cause serious bone problems, which could cause issues when colonists have to take long flights to their new home in **microgravity**. Scientists worry that the higher levels of **radiation** in space could also lead to major health problems for **space colonists**.

However, despite these issues, many scientists believe that space colonization can and will happen. It's just a matter of time!

Hi! I'm Robert Zubrin. I'm an American scientist with a passion for the idea of sending humans to Mars. I've set up a society where scientists from around the world can share their research and ideas about how humans could explore and settle on Mars. If we work together, we believe that people will be able to find a new permanent home on Mars, creating a new, exciting world for humankind!

THINK ABOUT IT!

Now that you know more about what life on another planet might be like, would you move to space if you could?

Conclusion

Earth is just one tiny planet in the unimaginable vastness of space. But as we've seen, it's very special in that its conditions are perfectly suited to life as we know it. So far, we haven't found any other world with these exact same conditions. But that hasn't stopped scientists from planning how we could live in space anyway!

Moving people to a new home in space would be a massive challenge. We still have a lot to learn about other planets and **moons.** The technology needed to get us to another world and keep us alive when we get there is a long way off. And let's not forget the unbelievable cost of a project like this!

FUN FACT!

Sending just the NASA Perseverance **rover** to Mars cost nearly $3 billion! Imagine how much it would cost to send humans there.

As technology and our understanding of our **solar system** and beyond improves, colonizing another planet in addition to Earth might become a possibility. A **space colony** could be used as a site for research and experiments, a base to further explore space, *and* as a backup in case something goes wrong back home!

I think we've got just enough for the space suits!

However, even with advances in science and technology, moving everyone on Earth to a new home in space would still be hugely difficult and expensive. It would definitely be cheaper, simpler, and easier to resolve the problems on Earth rather than just give up and move to another planet. Now is the time to solve issues such as **climate change** and pollution, so that future generations can still live safely and happily on our home planet.

Some scientists believe there are between 100 and 200 billion **galaxies** in the universe, so just imagine how many planets are out there! Maybe one day, we'll find another with the same conditions as Earth.

Thank you!

Generating electricity with wind turbines is much better for our planet than burning **fossil fuels.** It releases no pollution, and we will never run out of wind!

Summary

Living on another planet is unlikely to happen anytime soon, but it may one day become reality! Check your understanding of the information in this book.

Our planet becomes uninhabitable because of **climate change** and pollution.

We have to leave Earth because of a major natural disaster, such as an **asteroid** collision.

We use up all the essential resources on Earth.

We finally have the technology to plan a manned trip to another planet or body in space.

We send colonists to a new world in space. This could be Mars, Titan, or somewhere different.

In the long run, it might be possible to **terraform** our new home to make it more like Earth. This would make it possible for colonists to leave their habitats without space suits and even grow food directly in the soil.

THINK ABOUT IT!

Do you think it's likely that humans will visit or set up a colony on another planet during your lifetime? Why or why not?

Our **space colony** could be used as a base to explore new areas of our **solar system** and beyond.

First, space colonists would build protective habitats where they could live, sleep, work, and grow food to eat in greenhouses.

Eventually, **space colonists** could begin to extract such **resources** as fuel and building materials from their new home. They would be able to source everything they need locally.

Glossary

asteroid—a very large rock that orbits the sun

atmosphere—the gases around a planet or large body in space

climate change—changes in the world's weather, in particular an increase in temperature, which scientists believe are mainly due to human activity

comet—a body of rock and ice that orbits the sun at a great distance

crop—a plant grown for food, such as apples, carrots, or potatoes

drought—a long period with little or no rain

dwarf planet—a round body that orbits a star but isn't large enough to be considered a planet (sorry Pluto!)

element—one of the basic substances from which everything in the universe is made

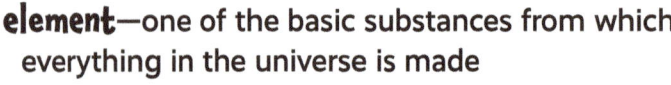

exoplanet—a planet outside our solar system

fossil fuel—a fuel, such as natural gas, oil, or coal, that was formed over millions of years from the remains of animals and plants

galaxy—a very large group of stars

global warming—an increase in temperatures on Earth due to the greenhouse effect

gravity—the force that attracts objects toward each other

hibernation—a long period of a sleeplike state in which you don't need to eat or drink

light-year—the distance that light travels in one year—an astonishing 5.88 trillion miles (9.46 trillion kilometers)!

magnetic field—the area around a magnet or something magnetic in which it can attract objects

microgravity—very weak gravity, as experienced in a spacecraft that is orbiting Earth

molecule—a very small amount of a chemical

moon—a round object that orbits a planet

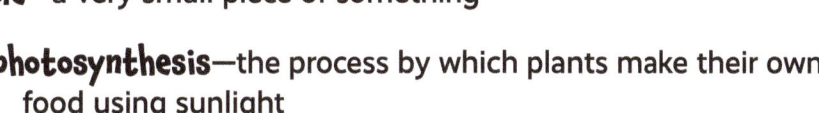

ore—rock or soil from which metal can be extracted

particle—a very small piece of something

photosynthesis—the process by which plants make their own food using sunlight

pressure—the force created by something pushing on something else

probe—an unmanned spacecraft that gathers data from space

radiation—a type of energy that can be dangerous to our health (eek!)

resource—a useful material

rover—a vehicle that can explore the surface of other planets

solar system—everything that orbits around a star (in our case, that's the sun!)

space colonist—someone who has settled on another planet or body in space

space colony—a human settlement on another planet or body in space

space station—a vehicle in which people can orbit Earth outside of its atmosphere

terraform—to change a planet to make it more similar to Earth

Review and reflect

COMPREHENSION QUESTIONS

Earth and space
- Why are scientists interested in studying exoplanets and other faraway places outside our solar system?

Getting started
- Why would space colonists need good protective gear and would likely spend the majority of their time inside habitats?

Doomsday dangers
- What are some of the serious threats that put our planet at risk of becoming uninhabitable?

Next steps
- According to the text, what is a major benefit of having a home somewhere else in space?

Where to go?
- What unique conditions does Earth have that allow for life?
- In addition to Mars, where else are scientists considering as potential sites for human colonization?

Long-term living
- How do the problem-solution-consequence diagrams on pages 36-37 help you consider the effects of humans colonizing Mars?
- What do we still need to learn about how the human body will cope with being in space?

Blast off!
- Describe the two options scientists have suggested as potential solutions to the problem that some space journeys would take significantly longer than most humans live.

Conclusion and summary
- After reading this book and considering what would happen if we had to live on other planets, what is your biggest takeaway? Why?

MAKE A CHAIN OF EVENTS!

Creating a paper chain can help you explore and visualize how cause and effect relationships can be thought of as a sequence of events.

You'll need:
- Pencil
- Scratch paper
- Pens or markers
- Stapler and staples
- Strips of paper (2 colors, if possible)

Instructions:

1. **Select a focus:** Choose a specific aspect from the book that caught your attention—it could be risks to our environment on Earth or problems with traveling to and living on another planet or body in space.

2. **Brainstorm causes and effects:** On a sheet of scratch paper, brainstorm and list the causes and effects related to your chosen focus. Think critically about the factors that contributed to or resulted from your focus. You can always look back in the text for ideas!

3. **Write on strips:** Write each cause and each effect on its own strip of paper. If you have different colored paper, use one color for the cause strips and the other for the effect strips.

4. **Create the paper chain:** Organize your strips into causes and effects. Start forming a paper chain to show how a cause leads to an effect. Use the stapler to connect the two strips. Continue adding cause and effect strips as links in your chain. When you've finished, you should be able to start at the beginning of your chain and read through each chain link in a logical order.

5. **Linking multiple chains:** If your focus has multiple causes or effects, you can create additional chains and link them together to show how complex cause and effect relationships can be!

Write about it!

Look at the paper chain you created and how the causes link to effects (which in turn link to other causes!). How might breaking a link in the chain impact the overall sequence of events?

World Book, Inc.
180 North LaSalle Street
Suite 900
Chicago, Illinois 60601
USA

For information about other World Book publications, visit our website at www.worldbook.com or call 1-800-WORLDBK (967-5325).

For information about sales to schools and libraries, call 1-800-975-3250 (United States), or 1-800-837-5365 (Canada).

© 2024 (print and e-book) by World Book, Inc. All rights reserved. No part of this publication may be reproduced, stored in a retrieval system, or transmitted in any form or by any means (electronic, mechanical, photocopying, recording, or otherwise) without written permission from World Book, Inc.

WORLD BOOK and the GLOBE DEVICE are registered trademarks or trademarks of World Book, Inc.

Library of Congress Cataloging-in-Publication Data for this volume has been applied for.

What Would Happen If...?
978-0-7166-5448-3 (set, hc.)

We Had to Live on Other Planets?
ISBN: 978-0-7166-5454-4 (hc.)

Also available as:

ISBN: 978-0-7166-5460-5 (e-book)
ISBN: 978-0-7166-5466-7 (soft cover)

Staff

Editorial

Vice President
Tom Evans

Editorial Project Coordinator
Kaile Kilner

Curriculum Designer
Caroline Davidson

Proofreader
Nathalie Strassheim

Graphics and Design

Senior Visual Communications Designer
Melanie Bender

Digital Asset Specialist
Rosalia Bledsoe

Written by Izzi Howell
Illustrated by Paula Bossio

Developed with World Book by
White-Thomson Publishing LTD
www.wtpub.co.uk

Acknowledgments

4-5   © 24Novembers/Shutterstock; CNSA; © NASA images/Shutterstock
6-7   © 19 STUDIO/Shutterstock; © Nerthuz/Shutterstock; NASA/JPL-Caltech; © NASA images/Shutterstock
8-9   ESA/Hubble, M. Kornmesser; NASA GSFC/CIL/Adriana Manrique Gutierrez
10-11   © John Carnemolla, Shutterstock; © huyangshu/Shutterstock
12-13   © Wirestock Creators/Shutterstock; © Piyaset/Shutterstock
14-15   © Goinyk Production/Shutterstock; © Tom Pfeiffer, Alamy Images
16-17   © leeborn/Shutterstock; © Aphelleon/Shutterstock; © Serg64/Shutterstock; © Juhku/Shutterstock; © Triff/Shutterstock
18-19   NASA/ESA/DLR/Freie Universitat Berlin (G. Neukum)
20-21   © Science History Images/Alamy Images; ESA/NASA/JPL/University of Arizona; © Science Photo Library/Alamy Images
22-23   NASA/Pat Rawlings (SAIC); © Vadim Sadovski, Shutterstock
24-25   © DM7/Alamy Images; Roscosmos/NASA
26-27   NASA; © Jamen Percy, Shutterstock
28-29   © Lili.Q/Shutterstock; © Emilia Stasiak, Shutterstock; © Neirfy/Shutterstock; NASA/Alexander Gerst
30-31   © Kitch Bain, Shutterstock; NASA; © Dundanim/Shutterstock; © paulista/Shutterstock; © Alones/Shutterstock
32-33   © Stocktrek Images, Inc./Alamy Images; ESA/Foster + Partners
34-35   © 24K-Production/Shutterstock; ESA
38-39   © dotted zebra/Alamy Images; © Stockbym/Shutterstock
41   © Giusparta/Shutterstock; © Antares_StarExplorer/Shutterstock
46-47   © Roi and Roi/Shutterstock